Instant Pot Cookbook for Beginners

Fun & Easy Instant Pot Recipes for Beginners

Instant Pot Cooking Made Easy
Book 9

By Brendan Fawn

ISBN: 9798642616901

Introduction

If you think about it in the long run, we are essentially living in an age where we are completely surrounded by technology in all aspects of our life. From our day to day life, to our living rooms and even our kitchens! Smart Gadgets are taking over everything and improving the quality of life for us.

And on the topic of kitchen gadgets, the culinary industry has, in reality, undergone a significant advancement in terms of modern and new gadgets that make the process of cooking a total breeze. Appliances and gadgets such as the Sous Vide circulators, Air Fryers, Slow Cookers are designed from the ground up to make the life of rising and experienced chefs easier.

Following that very trend, the now world-famous Instant Pot came into play and completely took the whole world by storm.

In a nutshell, Instant Pots are appliances that stand at the pinnacle of Electric Pressure Cookers and completely revolutionized the cooking industry. This is the most evolved version of a traditional pressure cooker.

This cookbook includes various Instant Pot recipes. In this cookbook, you will find interesting and mouth-watering Instant Pot recipes that will inspire you to cook delicious dishes.

Often you should just use your imagination because actually there are no limits. And remember, this cookbook hasn't all the recipes because it was created to inspire you to discover a colorful world of Instant Pot cooking!

Moreover, you don't need to be a professional 28 Michelin Star chef to use Instant Pot recipes from this cooking book and to prepare the food for yourself, your friends or your family.

So, without delaying any further, before letting you in on the recipes themselves, let me first talk a little bit about the Instant Pot itself.

What is Instant Pot

As mentioned in the section above, Instant Pot's are possibly the most advanced Electric Pressure Cookers out there. But you must be wondering, what exactly makes them so special?

Well, the Instant Pot is essentially a 7 in 1 device that has the potential to be used as a yogurt maker, food steamer, baker, gravy maker, and even a sauté pan! But that's not all to be honest, with a little bit of creativity, the list goes on.

Since the conception of the very first Instant Pot, there have been multiple models out there in the market, each designed to cater to a particular type of audience.

While the core functionalities of all of these pots remaining the same, they stand out from the group by having some model-specific features.

Below is a breakdown of some of the most common models available.

LUX

The Lux line of Instant Pot is probably the cheapest one with fewer features when compared to its bigger brothers. However, this is a good option if you are having second thoughts but still want to give the device a shot.

At the time of writing, this model had a price tag of 79$.

DUO

This is the most popular Instant Pot model that boasts a 6-quart capacity and combines the versatility of being able to have a pressure cooker, rice cooker, slow cooker, steamer, yogurt maker, Sauté/browning functionality, etc. in a single device.

There are 14 different functions in total, and the device allows you to cook at HIGH or LOW pressures, which gives you further control over your meals.

At the time of writing, this model had a price tag of 99$.

DUO PLUS

This is the updated model of the DUO and it comes packed with additional features such as Cake, Egg and Sterilize settings. Aesthetics of the display is updated as well with a convenient blue LCD. The inner pot of the device has also seen some updates as well.

At the time of writing, this model had a price tag of 110-125$.

ULTRA

The Ultra variant of the Instant Pot comes in only 6 and 8-quart sizes. This device has a unique dial that allows you to make adjustments for custom cook settings.

Not only that! The Ultra also comes packed with a built-in altitude adjustment meter and an in-depth display, both of which helps to make the cooking process much more accessible, even in high altitude places.

At the time of writing, this model had a price tag of 149.99-159.99$.

SMART BLUETOOTH

The Smart Bluetooth variant is the most advanced Instant Pot model to date and is designed to cater to the tech enthusiasts out there.
This particular model comes packed with all the features of the Instant Pot Duo but with added Bluetooth capability.
At the time of writing, this model had a price tag of 159.99$.

How to Use the Instant Pot Buttons

Some people often think that due to the plethora of functionalities available to the Instant Pot, using the device might feel a little bit jarring and difficult.
Let me assure you now, that this is nothing more than a mere misconception! Using the Instant Pot is extremely easy, and even an amateur cook can utilize it to its full potential. The only catch is that you must know what all the different buttons of the pot do.
This section is dedicated to just that. Below is a breakdown of all the core buttons of the Instant Pot, do give this is a read in order to better understand all the different functionalities of the pot itself.

Sauté: You should go for this button if you want to sauté your vegetables or meat inside your inner pot while keeping the lid open. It is possible to adjust the level of brownness you desire by pressing the modify button as well. As a small tip here, you can very quickly push the Sauté Button followed by the Adjust Button two times to simmer your food.

Keep Warm/Cancel: Using this button, you will be able to turn your pressure cooker off. Alternatively, you can use the adjust button to keep maintaining a warm temperature ranging from 293 degrees F (on average) to 332 degrees F (at more) degrees Celsius depending on what you need.

Manual: This is pretty much an all-rounder button which gives a higher level of flexibility to the user. Using this button followed by the + or − buttons, you will be able to set the exact duration of cooking time which you require.

Soup: This mode will set the cooker to a high-pressure mode giving 30 minutes of cooking time (at normal); 40 minutes (at more); 20 minutes (at less)

Meat/Stew: This mode will set the cooker to a high-pressure mode giving 35 minutes of cooking time (at normal); 45 minutes (at more); 20 minutes (at less)

Bean/Chili: This mode will set the cooker to a high-pressure mode giving 30 minutes of cooking time (at normal); 40 minutes (at more); 25 minutes (at less)

Poultry: This mode will set the cooker to a high-pressure mode giving 15 minutes of cooking time (at normal); 30 minutes (at more); 5 minutes (at less)

Rice: This is a fully automated mode that cooks rice at low pressure. It will adjust the timer all by itself depending on the amount of water/rice present in the inner cooking pot.

Multi-Grain: This mode will set the cooker to a high-pressure mode giving 40 minutes of cooking time (at normal); 45 minutes (at more); 20 minutes (at less)

Porridge: This mode will set the cooker to a high-pressure mode giving 20 minutes of cooking time (at normal); 30 minutes (at more); 15 minutes (at less)

Steam: This will set your pressure cooker to high pressure with 10 minutes of cooking time at normal. 15 minutes cook time at more and 3 minutes cook time at less. Keep in mind that it is advised to use this model with a steamer basket or rack for best results.

Slow Cooker: This button will normally set the cooker at 4-hour mode. However, you change the temperature by keeping it at 190-201 Fahrenheit (at low); 194-205 degrees Fahrenheit (at normal); 199-210 degrees Fahrenheit (at high);

Pressure: This button allows you to alter between high and low-pressure settings.

Yogurt: This setting should be used when you are in the mood for making yogurt in individual pots or jars

Timer: This button will allow you to either decrease or increase the time by using the timer button and pressing the + or − buttons.

All of the recipes in this book are made using very simple and easy to find ingredients and are perfect for small groups of 3 or 4 people. You will meat, seafood and fish recipes in this cookbook.
But advanced chefs fear not! As in between the simpler ones, you might stumble upon a few harder recipes that will teach you a new thing or two. All said, this book essentially has something for everyone.
With that, I encourage you to start exploring the recipes and embark on your Instant Pot quest!

Chapter 1: Instant Pot Lunch Recipes

Instant Beef Burgers

Serving: 2
Prep Time: 10 minutes
Cooking Time: 55 minutes
Ingredients:

- 1 pound ground beef
- 2 buns halved
- 2 tomatoes, sliced
- 2 marinated cucumbers, sliced
- 1 white onion, peeled and sliced
- 3 tablespoons soy sauce
- 1 tablespoon dry basil
- 4 garlic cloves, minced
- 4 tablespoons mayonnaise
- salt and black pepper, to taste
- fresh parsley

How to Prepare:

1. In a bowl, combine the garlic, basil, salt and pepper with the ground beef and mix well. Then set the beef aside to marinate it for at least few hours unrefrigerated at room temperature.

2. Preheat the oven to 250°-270°Fahrenheit and roast the buns in the oven for 10 minutes until lightly browned and crispy and then set aside.
3. Form the meat chops. Add in the meat to your Pot and close the lid to cook on MEAT/STEW mode. Remember to set the timer to 45 minutes._Release the pressure over 10 minutes. Prepare the burgers with the beef chops, mayonnaise and vegetables.
4. Serve with the fresh parsley and cold beer!

<u>Nutrition (Per Serving):</u>
Calories: 301; Fat: 64g; Carbohydrates: 221g; Protein: 51g

Spicy Rendang Beef

Serving: 4
Prep Time: 20 minutes
Cook Time: 55 minutes

Ingredients:

- 15 oz beef, cubed
- 2 lemons, peeled and cubed
- 2 onions, peeled and chopped
- 1 tablespoon of ginger, minced
- 1 small jalapeno pepper, chopped
- 5 tablespoons sunflower oil
- 4 garlic cloves, minced
- 1 pack of rendang curry paste
- ½ a cup of water

How to Prepare:

1. In a bowl, combine the onions, jalapeno pepper, garlic, ginger and rendang curry paste. Toss the beef in the spices and vegetables mix. Then set the meat aside to marinate it for at least few hours unrefrigerated at room temperature or place in the fridge overnight.
2. Set your Instant Pot to sauté mode and add in the sunflower oil and lemons.
3. Allow the oil to heat up and add the beef and all the remaining ingredients. Pour the water and close the lid to cook on a HIGH pressure for 55 minutes.
4. Serve with the beer and vegetables salad.

Nutrition (Per Serving):

Calories: 326; Fat: 68g; Carbohydrates: 259g; Protein: 58g

Goose with Pineapples

Servings: 4
Prep Time: 20 minutes
Cooking Time: 75 minutes

Ingredients:

- 1 goose
- 1 cup of pistachios
- 10 oz pineapples, peeled and diced
- 2 medium onions, peeled and chopped
- 6 cloves garlic, minced
- 2 teaspoons chili powder
- 3 teaspoons oregano
- 1 teaspoon cumin powder
- 5 tablespoons Olive oil
- 2 cups of tomatoes, chopped
- 2 cups of chicken broth
- 2 teaspoons nutmeg
- Salt and pepper to taste

How to Prepare:

1. Combine the salt, nutmeg, cumin, oregano, garlic, pistachios and black pepper. Season the goose with the spices mix. Spoon the pineapple cubes and mix well. Then set the goose aside to marinate for at least few hours unrefrigerated at room temperature.
2. In a skillet or wok, heat the Olive oil and fry the chopped onions for around 10 minutes until clear and caramelized.
3. Set your Instant Pot to sauté mode and add in the Olive oil to heat it up.
4. Spoon the goose and stir for 5 minutes.
5. Mix in the onions and sauté until fragrant, then spoon all the remaining ingredients and mix well.
6. Close the lid and cook for 50 minutes on a HIGH pressure and then release the pressure over 10 minutes.
7. Cut the goose and serve with the white wine.

Nutrition (Per Serving):

Calories: 331; Fat: 71g; Carbohydrates: 252g; Protein: 51g

Spicy Goose with Potato Purée

Servings: 4
Prep Time: 20 minutes
Cooking Time: 85 minutes

Ingredients:

- 40 oz goose
- 5 oz potatoes
- 1 cup of milk
- 2 medium onions, peeled and chopped
- 6 cloves garlic, minced
- 2 teaspoons chili powder
- 3 teaspoons oregano
- 1 teaspoon cumin powder
- 5 oz sunflower oil
- 2 cups of tomatoes, chopped
- 2 cups of chicken broth
- 2 teaspoons nutmeg
- Salt and pepper to taste
- 2 tablespoons basil

How to Prepare:
1. Combine the salt, nutmeg, cumin, oregano, garlic and black pepper. Season the goose with the spices mix. Then set the goose aside to marinate for at least few hours unrefrigerated at room temperature or place in the fridge overnight.
2. Heat the Olive oil and fry the chopped onions for around 10 minutes until clear and caramelized.
3. Set your Instant Pot to sauté mode and add in the sunflower oil to heat it up.
4. Spoon the goose and stir for 5 minutes.
5. Mix in the onions and sauté until fragrant, then spoon all the remaining ingredients and mix well.
6. Close the lid and cook for 50 minutes on a HIGH pressure and then release the pressure naturally over 10 minutes.
7. Meanwhile, heat the water and boil the potatoes on a medium heat for around 20 minutes. Then heat the milk and mash the potatoes with the milk using the potato masher.
8. Then slice the goose and portion with the potato purée into four plates. Top each plate with the basil. Remember that this dish should be served warm. Serve it with the red or white wine and enjoy!

Nutrition (Per Serving):
Calories: 344; Fat: 70g; Carbohydrates: 259g; Protein: 60g

Duck with Caramel and Pimpkin

Serving: 4
Prep Time: 10 minutes
Cooking Time: 60 minutes

Ingredients:

- 30 oz of duck
- 1 cup of pumpkin, diced
- 3 tablespoons caramel
- 5 tablespoons Olive oil
- 1 tablespoon ranch dressing
- 1 jar of pepper rings
- 1 tablespoon of Italian seasoning
- 10 tablespoons unsalted butter
- 1 cup of water
- 4 teaspoons basil

How to Prepare:

1. Set your Instant Pot to sauté mode and add in 1 tablespoon Olive oil.
2. Once the oil is hot, add the duck and sear both sides.
3. Then turn the sauté mode off and pour the water, add in the Italian seasoning mix, basil, unsalted butter, pumpkin, caramel and pepper rings on top of your duck.
4. Close the lid and cook for 60 minutes on a MEDIUM pressure.
5. Release the pressure naturally over 10 minutes.
6. Then cut the duck and portion it into four plates and top each plate with the basil. Remember that this dish should be served warm. Serve it with the red or white wine.

Nutrition (Per Serving):
Calories: 371; Fat: 69g; Carbohydrates: 251g; Protein: 52g

Chicken Livers with Carrots and Onions

Servings: 4
Prep Time: 20 minutes
Cooking Time: 65 minutes

Ingredients:

- 40 oz chicken livers
- 1 cup of milk
- 1 cup of walnuts
- 10 onions, peeled and chopped
- 4 medium carrots, peeled and chopped
- 6 cloves garlic, minced
- 2 teaspoons chili powder
- 3 teaspoons oregano
- 1 teaspoon cumin powder
- 5 oz sunflower oil
- 2 cups of tomatoes, chopped
- 2 cups of chicken broth
- 2 teaspoons nutmeg
- Salt and pepper to taste

How to Prepare:
1. Soak the chicken livers in the milk for around 5 hours.
2. Preheat the oven to 250°-270°Fahrenheit and roast the walnuts in the oven for 10 minutes until lightly browned and crispy and then set aside to cool completely. Then grind the walnuts using a food processor or blender.
3. Combine the salt, nutmeg, cumin, oregano, garlic, walnuts and black pepper. Season the chicken liver with the spices mix. Then set the chicken liver aside to marinate for at least few hours unrefrigerated at room temperature or place in the fridge overnight.
4. Heat the Olive oil and fry the chopped onions and carrots for around 10 minutes until clear and caramelized.
5. Set your Instant Pot to sauté mode and add in the sunflower oil to heat it up.
6. Spoon the chicken livers and stir for 5 minutes.
7. Mix in the onions and sauté until fragrant, then spoon all the remaining ingredients and mix well.

8. Close the lid and cook for 40 minutes on a MEDIUM pressure
and then release the pressure naturally over 10 minutes.
9. Serve with the white wine and enjoy!

<u>Nutrition (Per Serving):</u>
Calories: 345; Fat: 71g; Carbohydrates: 251g; Protein: 54g

Smoked Beef Sausages with Shrimps and Noodles

Serving: 4
Prep Time: 10 minutes
Cook Time: 60 minutes
<u>**Ingredients:**</u>

- 6 medium smoked beef sausages around 35 oz
- 2 cups of small shrimps
- 35 oz noodles
- 3 cups of water
- 1 medium onion, peeled and chopped
- 2 garlic cloves, minced
- 1 bouillon cube
- 2 tablespoons sunflower oil
- 1 teaspoon of cumin
- kosher salt, to taste
- black pepper, to taste

How to Prepare:

1. Cut the beef sausages into the rings and fry them with the shrimps for around 10 minutes until golden brown and crispy.
2. Boil the water to cook the noodles for 10 minutes until half-cooked.

3. Set your Instant Pot to sauté mode and pour some sunflower oil. Add in the garlic and onions to sauté for 5 minutes until clear and caramelized.

4. Set your Instant Pot to the WARM mode and add in all the remaining ingredients. Close the lid and cook for 35 minutes on a HIGH pressure.

5. Release the pressure naturally over 10 minutes.

6. Portion the beef sausages and noodles into four bowls or mugs and dollop each bowl with the shrimps.

<u>Nutrition (Per Serving):</u> Calories: 341; Fat: 41g; Carbohydrates: 59g; Protein: 32g

Spicy Turkey and Bean Rice

Serving: 4
Prep Time: 10 minutes
Cook Time: 65 minutes

Ingredients:

- 30 oz turkey, cubed
- 2 cups of brown rice
- 2 cups of red beans
- 3 cups of water
- 1 medium onion, peeled and chopped
- 1 yellow pepper, peeled and diced
- 2 garlic cloves, minced
- 1 bouillon cube
- 2 tablespoons sunflower oil
- 1 tablespoon chili powder
- ½ a teaspoon of cayenne pepper
- 1 teaspoon of cumin
- Salt and pepper

How to Prepare:

1. Combine the chili powder, cumin, cayenne pepper, salt and pepper. Season the turkey with the spices and set it aside to marinate for at least few hours unrefrigerated at room temperature or place in the fridge overnight.
2. Soak the red beans in the warm water for overnight and then heat the water and boil the beans for around 10 minutes until half-cooked.
3. Wash the brown rice several times and boil the water to cook the rice for 10 minutes until half-cooked.
4. Set your Instant Pot to sauté mode and pour some sunflower oil. Add in the garlic and onions, to sauté for 5 minutes until clear and caramelized.
5. Set your Instant Pot to the WARM mode and add in the remaining ingredients (except the yellow pepper).
6. Close the lid and cook for 40 minutes on a HIGH pressure.
7. Release the pressure naturally over 10 minutes.
8. Portion the turkey, beans and rice into four bowls or mugs and dollop each bowl with the yellow pepper cubes. Remember that

this dish should be served warm. Serve the spicy turkey, beans and rice with the red wine.

Nutrition (Per Serving)
Calories: 272; Fat: 30g; Carbohydrates: 52g; Protein: 25g

Chicken Sausages with Croutons

Serving: 2
Prep Time: 10 minute
Cooking Time: 50 minutes

Ingredients:

- 4 medium (10-12 oz) chicken sausages
- 5 carrots, peeled and diced
- 2 baguettes
- 8 gloves of garlic, minced
- 2 teaspoons garlic powder
- 5 tablespoons unsalted butter
- 1 cup of cream
- 1 cup of water
- Salt and pepper to taste

How to Prepare:

1. Cut the sausages into rings. In a skillet, heat the butter and fry the sausages rings for 10-15 minutes until golden brown.
2. Cut the baguettes into small cubes and toss them with the salt and garlic powder. Preheat the oven to 240°-260° Fahrenheit and spread the baguette cubes on a baking sheet. Bake the croutons for 10-15 minutes until golden brown and crispy.
3. Add the water to your Instant Pot and place the steamer rack at the bottom of your pot.
4. Place the carrots, sausages, garlic, butter and all the remaining ingredients in a steamer basket and place them on top of the steamer rack and close the lid to cook on a HIGH pressure for 15-20 minutes.
5. Quick-release the pressure and let the sausages to cool. Spoon the croutons and mix well.
6. Portion the carrots and sausages with the croutons into few bowls or mugs. Remember that this dish should be served warm. Serve the dish with the beer.

Nutrition (Per Serving):
Calories: 204; Fat: 35g; Carbohydrates: 36g; Protein: 29g

Spicy Beef Steak

Serving: 4
Prep Time: 10 minutes
Cooking Time: 65 minutes

Ingredients:

- 40 oz beef steaks
- 2 cups of mayonnaise
- 1/3 cup green pitted olives + 2 tablespoons brine
- 1 small red pepper, chopped
- 1 cup of water
- 8 garlic cloves, minced
- 2 tablespoons garlic powder
- 4 medium onions, peeled and chopped
- 1 and ¾ teaspoon garlic salt
- 5 tablespoons sunflower oil
- Black pepper to taste

How to Prepare:

1. Combine the garlic, garlic powder, salt, black pepper, onion and pepper. Season the beef with the spices and vegetables mix. Then toss the beef in the mayonnaise and set it aside to marinate for at least few hours unrefrigerated at room temperature or place in the fridge overnight.

2. In a skillet or wok, heat the oil and fry the onions for around 10 minutes until clear and caramelized.
3. Add the beef to the Pot and mix in the rest of the ingredients.
4. Close the lid and cook the beef for around 55 minutes on a HIGH pressure.
5. Release the pressure naturally over 10 minutes.
6. Portion the beef steaks and serve with the orange juice and mayonnaise.

Nutrition (Per Serving):
Calories: 371; Fat: 79g; Carbohydrates: 262g; Protein: 64g

Goose with Walnuts and Plums

Serving: 4
Prep Time: 10 minutes
Cooking Time: 50 minutes

Ingredients:

- 1 medium goose, cubed
- 2 cups of walnuts
- 2 cups of dried plums
- 1 tablespoon Olive oil
- 1 teaspoon salt
- 1 teaspoon ground black pepper
- 1 teaspoon onion powder
- 1 teaspoon garlic powder
- 4 cups of vegetables broth
- fresh greenery

How to Prepare:
1. Preheat the oven to 250°-270°Fahrenheit and roast the walnuts in the oven for 10 minutes until lightly browned and crispy and then set aside.
2. Place the goose into the Instant Pot and season it well with the salt and pepper, mix well.
3. Add the oil and set the pot to sauté mode, sear each side of the goose for 10 minutes until slightly browned and crispy.
4. Pour the vegetables broth; add in the onion powder, walnuts, plums, garlic powder and all the remaining ingredients. Mix well.
5. Close the lid and cook on a HIGH pressure for 40 minutes.
6. Once the timer goes off release the pressure over 10 minutes to open the lid.
7. Then portion the goose into four plates and top each plate with the fresh greenery. Remember that this dish should be served warm. Serve it with the red or white wine.

Nutrition (Per Serving):
Calories: 278; Fat: 78g; Carbohydrates: 258g; Protein: 57g

Beef Liver with Pineapple and Orange

Servings: 4
Prep Time: 20 minutes
Cooking Time: 65 minutes
Ingredients:

- 35 oz beef liver
- 1 cup of pistachios
- 1 cup of pineapples, diced
- 1 cup of orange juice
- 2 medium onions, peeled and chopped
- 6 cloves garlic, minced
- 2 teaspoons chili powder
- 3 teaspoons oregano
- 1 teaspoon cumin powder
- 5 tablespoons Olive oil
- 2 cups of tomatoes, chopped
- 2 cups of chicken broth
- 2 teaspoons nutmeg
- Salt and pepper to taste

How to Prepare:
1. Combine the salt, nutmeg, cumin, oregano, garlic, pistachios and black pepper. Season the beef liver with the spices mix. Then set the liver aside to marinate for at least few hours unrefrigerated at room temperature or place in the fridge overnight. Cube the liver.
2. In a skillet or wok, heat the Olive oil and fry the chopped onions for around 10 minutes until clear and caramelized.
3. Set your Instant Pot to sauté mode and add in the Olive oil to heat it up.
4. Spoon the liver and stir for 5 minutes.
5. Mix in the onions and sauté until fragrant, then spoon all the remaining ingredients and mix well. Pour the orange juice
6. Close the lid and cook for 50 minutes on a MEDIUM pressure and then release the pressure over 10 minutes.
7. Serve with the white wine and enjoy!

Nutrition (Per Serving):
Calories: 371; Fat: 70g; Carbohydrates: 265g; Protein: 54g

Chapter 2: Instant Pot Seafood Recipes

Shrimps Bouillon with Leek

Serving: 4
Prep Time: 10 minutes
Cooking Time: 60 minutes

Ingredients:

- 30 oz medium shrimps
- 1 medium leek, chopped
- 1 chili pepper
- 3 tablespoons frozen vegetable mix
- 5 cups of water
- 3 teaspoons basil, dried and crushed
- 1/8 teaspoon oregano, crushed
- ½ medium onion, chopped
- 4 garlic cloves, minced
- sea salt and black pepper, to taste

How to Prepare:
1. Add all the ingredients to the Instant Pot and mix well.
2. Close the lid and select the slow mode to cook for 60 minutes.

3. Keep the pressure and then release the handle to the Venting position.

4. Once cooked, stir the bouillon well.

5. Portion the bouillon into four bowls or mugs. Remember that this dish should be served warm.

Nutrition (Per Serving):
Calories: 269; Fat: 56g; Carbohydrates: 185g; Protein: 42g

Salmon with Eggs Salad

Serving: 3
Prep Time: 15 minutes
Cook Time: 45 minutes
<u>Ingredients:</u>

- 15 oz salmon
- 3 eggs
- 5 tablespoons mayonnaise
- 1 big, white onion, peeled and chopped
- 1 bunch of fresh parsley, chopped
- 3 garlic cloves, smashed
- 1 teaspoon paprika
- 1 teaspoon oregano
- 2 tablespoons Olive oil
- 1 teaspoon dried rosemary
- salt and pepper, to taste

<u>How to Prepare:</u>

1. In a bowl, combine the salt, pepper, garlic, paprika, dried rosemary and oregano. Toss the salmon in the spices mix and pour the white wine over the fish. Then set the fish aside to marinate for at least few hours unrefrigerated at room temperature or place in the fridge overnight.
2. Place the fish into the steamer basket and lower into the liquid.
3. Close the lid and cook for 35 minutes on a HIGH pressure.
4. Quick-release the pressure.
5. Heat the water and boil the eggs for around 10 minutes. Chop the eggs.
6. Open the lid and place the salmon on the cutting board and slice the fish.
7. In a bowl, combine all the ingredients and mix well, adding some mayonnaise.
8. Portion the fish salad into three plates and dollop each plate with the cooking sauce and some rosemary.

<u>Nutrition (Per Serving):</u>
Calories: 251; Fat: 38g; Carbohydrates: 161g; Protein: 40g

Sea Fish Bouillon with Onions and Leek

Serving: 4
Prep Time: 10 minutes
Cooking Time: 60 minutes
Ingredients:

- 2 codes, cut into pieces
- 1 Pacific halibut, cut into pieces
- 1 leek, chopped
- 1 bay leaf
- 5 cups of water
- 3 teaspoons basil, dried and crushed
- 1/8 teaspoon oregano, crushed
  4 medium onions, peeled and chopped
- 4 garlic cloves, minced
- 1 teaspoon sea salt
- 2 teaspoons black pepper
- 1 bunch of parsley, chopped

How to Prepare:
1. Heat the oil and fry the chopped onions and the leek on a low heat for around 10 minutes until clear and caramelized.
2. Add in all the ingredients to the Instant Pot and mix well.
3. Close the lid and select the slow mode to cook for 60 minutes.
4. Keep the pressure and then release the handle to the Venting position.
5. Once cooked, stir the bouillon well.
6. Portion the bouillon into four bowls or mugs. Remember that this dish should be served warm.

Nutrition (Per Serving):
Calories: 261; Fat: 48g; Carbohydrates: 162g; Protein: 37g

Shrimps Bouillon with Lime Juice

Serving: 4
Prep Time: 10 minutes
Cooking Time: 35 minutes
Ingredients:

- 2 cups of shrimps, cleaned and deveined
- 4 tablespoon sunflower oil
- ½ cup of lime juice
- 1 bunch of dill, chopped
- 2 bay leaves
- 2 teaspoons chili pepper powder
- 1 medium onion, thinly sliced
- 1 green bell pepper, thinly sliced
- 2 cloves garlic, smashed
- salt and pepper as needed
- 12 littleneck clams
- ¼ cup cilantro for garnish

How to Prepare:

1. Set your Instant Pot to sauté mode and add some sunflower oil.
2. Add the bay leaves and chili pepper powder and sauté for 5 minutes.

3. Add in the onion, bell pepper, 2 tablespoons of cilantro, garlic and season with the salt and pepper. Stir for few minutes and add in the lime juice.
4. Spoon all the remaining ingredients to the Instant Pot and place the shrimps on top.
5. Close the lid and cook on a HIGH pressure for 30 minutes. Release the pressure over 10 minutes. Portion the soup into four bowls or mugs and dollop each bowl with the chopped dill. Remember that this dish should be served warm.

<u>Nutrition (Per Serving):</u>
Calories: 244; Fat: 44g; Carbohydrates: 181g; Protein: 40g

Quinoa and Mackerel

Serving: 3
Prep Time: 15 minutes
Cook Time: 60 minutes

Ingredients:

- 3 mackerels
- 2 cups of quinoa
- 1 bunch of fresh parsley, chopped
- 1 cup of white wine
- 3 garlic cloves, smashed
- 1 teaspoon paprika
- 1 teaspoon oregano
- 2 tablespoons Olive oil
- 1 teaspoon dried rosemary
- salt and pepper, to taste

How to Prepare:

1. Soak the quinoa in the warm water for about 10 minutes. Boil the water to cook the quinoa for about 20 minutes or follow the cooking time suggested on the packet. Add 2 tablespoons Olive oil when the quinoa is ready.
2. In a bowl, combine the salt, pepper, garlic, paprika, dried rosemary and oregano. Toss the mackerels in the spices mix and pour the white wine over the fish. Then set the fish aside to marinate for at least few hours unrefrigerated at room temperature or place in the fridge overnight.
3. Place the mackerels into the steamer basket and lower into the liquid.
4. Close the lid and cook on a HIGH pressure for 40 minutes.
5. Quick-release the pressure.
6. Portion the mackerels and quinoa into three plates and dollop each plate with the cooking sauce and some rosemary. Serve the fish with the quinoa. Remember that this dish should be served warm.

Nutrition (Per Serving):
Calories: 262; Fat: 42g; Carbohydrates: 174g; Protein: 41g

Spicy Instant Tuna with Cashews

Serving: 4
Prep Time: 10 minutes
Cook Time: 55 minutes

Ingredients:

- 4 tuna fillets
- 2 cups of cashews
- 5 tablespoons squeezed lemon
- 1 teaspoon black pepper
- 1 teaspoon of white pepper
- 1 teaspoon of cayenne pepper
- 5 diced tomatoes
- 1 jalapeno pepper, minced
- 2 garlic cloves, peeled and minced
- 1 sweet onion, peeled and chopped
- 1 cup of water
- Sea salt
- 10 basil leaves, chopped

How to Prepare:

1. Preheat the oven to 250°-270°Fahrenheit and roast the cashews in the oven for 10 minutes until lightly browned and crispy and then set aside.
2. In a bowl, combine the tomatoes and basil. Spoon the tomatoes into your Instant Pot.
3. In a skillet, fry the onions and garlic on a low heat for around 10 minutes until clear and caramelized.
4. Marinate the tuna fillets in the salt, black, white and cayenne pepper for at least few hours unrefrigerated at room temperature. Sprinkle some lemon juice on top.
5. Pour the water and add the tuna and all the remaining ingredients (except the nuts) into the Instant Pot and close the lid.
6. Cook for 45 minutes on a MEDIUM pressure.
7. Perform quick release and serve with the cashews mix and rice.

Nutrition (Per Serving):

Calories: 241; Fat: 39g; Carbohydrates: 156g; Protein: 38g

Instant Fish Burgers

Serving: 3
Prep Time: 10 minutes
Cooking Time: 55 minutes

Ingredients:

- 6 fish chops
- 6 buns halved
- 2 tomatoes, sliced
- 4 oz lettuce
- 2 oz cheese
- 1 white onion, peeled and sliced
- 4 garlic cloves, minced
- 4 tablespoons mayonnaise
- black pepper, to taste

How to Prepare:

1. Preheat the oven to 250°-270°Fahrenheit and roast the buns in the oven for 10 minutes until lightly browned and crispy and then set aside.
2. Add the fish chops to your Pot and close the lid to cook on MEAT/STEW mode. Remember to set the timer to 25 minutes.

3. Release the pressure over 10 minutes. Prepare the burgers with the fish chops, mayonnaise and vegetables. Add some pepper to taste.

4. Serve with the cold beer!

<u>Nutrition (Per Serving):</u>
Calories: 255; Fat: 59g; Carbohydrates: 215g; Protein: 44g

Spicy Shrimps in Lime Sauce

Serving: 3
Prep Time: 10 minutes
Cook Time: 40 minutes

Ingredients:

- 20 oz shrimps
- 3 cups of water
- black pepper and salt, to taste

Sauce

- 1 jalapeno pepper, seeded and diced
- 2 medium limes
- 3 garlic cloves, minced
- 2 tablespoons sunflower oil
- 2 tablespoons hot water
- 1 chili pepper, chopped
- 1 tablespoon fresh parsley, chopped
- 1 teaspoon cumin

How to Prepare:

1. Halve the limes and then squeeze them.
2. In a bowl, combine all the listed sauce ingredients and mix well.
3. Combine all the sauce ingredients and mix well. Marinate the shrimps in the sauce for at least few hours unrefrigerated at room temperature. Add in the water into the Instant Pot and place the shrimps on a steam rack. Then place the shrimps inside your Instant Pot. Mix in all the remaining ingredients.
4. Close the lid and cook on a HIGH pressure for 40 minutes.
5. Release the pressure naturally over 10 minutes.
6. Open the lid and portion the shrimps into three plates and dollop each plate with the salt and pepper. Remember that this dish should be served warm. Serve the shrimps with the wine.

Nutrition (Per Serving):
Calories: 231; Fat: 41g; Carbohydrates: 164g; Protein: 38g

Cod with Oranges and Pineapple

Serving: 3
Prep Time: 10 minutes
Cooking Time: 20 minutes

Ingredients:

- 20 oz cod
- 1 cup of pistachio
- 2 oranges, peeled and diced
- 1 medium pineapple, diced
- 1 cup of white onion, peeled and chopped
- 2 bunches of parsley, chopped
- salt as needed
- Pepper as needed

How to Prepare:

1. Preheat the oven to 240°-260°Fahrenheit and roast the pistachio nuts in the oven for 10 minutes until lightly browned and crispy and then set aside to cool completely. Then grind the pistachio using a food processor or blender.
2. Marinate the cod with the pineapple for around 2 hours.
3. Add a cup of water to your Instant Pot and place a steamer rack.
4. Add in the cod to your Pot and mix in all the remaining ingredients (except the parsley). Then close the lid.
5. Cook on a HIGH pressure for 20 minutes.
6. Quick release the pressure.
7. Portion the cod into three plates and dollop each plate with the pistachio and parsley. Remember that this dish should be served warm. Serve the cod with the white wine.

Nutrition (Per Serving):

Calories: 240; Fat: 50g; Carbohydrates: 168g; Protein: 44g

Flatfish Fillets with Herbs Butter Sauce

Serving: 1
Prep Time: 10 minutes
Cooking Time: 45 minutes

Ingredients:

- 1 flatfish fillet
- 1 onion, peeled and chopped
- 2 bunches of parsley, chopped
- 10 oz herbs butter, cubed
- 3 tablespoons powdered garlic
- 2 tablespoon of Olive oil
- 1 bunch of dill, chopped
- Salt and pepper, to taste
- 1 lemon, halved

How to Prepare:

1. Add a cup of water to your Instant Pot and place a steamer rack.
2. Toss the flatfish fillet in the salt, pepper and powdered garlic. Sprinkle some lemon juice and marinate the fish for at least 1 hour.
3. Place the fillet to your Pot and close the lid.
4. Cook on a MEDIUM pressure for 45 minutes.

5. Place the flatfish fillet into the plate and dollop the fillet with the dill and parsley. In a skillet, melt the herbs butter.
6. Pour the melted herbs butter over the fish. Remember that this dish should be served warm.

<u>Nutrition (Per Serving):</u>
Calories: 234; Fat: 42g; Carbohydrates: 165g; Protein: 42g

Shrimps with Coconut

Serving: 4
Prep Time: 15 minutes
Cooking Time: 55 minutes
Ingredients:

- 2 pounds medium shrimps
- 5 garlic cloves, minced
- 1 cup of walnuts
- 1 cup of coconut milk
- 1 teaspoon creole seasoning
- 1 teaspoon parsley, dried
- 4 teaspoons sesame seeds oil
- 2 medium lemons
- 3 teaspoons soy sauce (low sodium)
- 1 cup of water

How to Prepare:
1. Preheat the oven to 240°-260°Fahrenheit and roast the walnuts in the oven for 10 minutes until lightly browned and crispy and then set aside to cool completely. Then grind the walnuts using a food processor or blender.
2. Meanwhile, halve the lemons and then squeeze them.
3. Add the sesame seeds oil to the Instant Pot and set it to the sauté mode, let it heat up.
4. Add the shrimps and garlic to your Instant Pot and sauté for 5-10 minutes.
5. In a bowl, combine the creole seasoning, dried parsley and soy sauce, mix well.
6. Pour the water and the coconut milk to your Instant Pot and spoon in all the ingredients (except the walnuts) on top of the shrimps.
7. Close the lid and cook for 35 minutes on a HIGH pressure.
8. Release the pressure naturally over 10 minutes.
9. Open the lid and portion the shrimps into four plates or bowls and sprinkle each plate with the lemon juice and walnuts. Remember that this dish should be served warm.

Nutrition (Per Serving):
Calories: 235; Fat: 42g; Carbohydrates: 165g; Protein: 42g

Salmon Heads Soup with Spanish Herbs and Lemon

Serving: 4
Prep Time: 15 minutes
Cooking Time: 70 minutes

Ingredients:

- 6 salmon heads
- 4 tablespoon sunflower oil
- 3 lemons, halved
- 2 teaspoons chili pepper powder
- 1 medium onion, thinly sliced
- 2 garlic cloves, smashed
- salt and pepper, to taste
- 1 cup of fish stock
- 5 cups of water
- ¼ cup of cilantro for garnish
- 1 teaspoon rosemary
- 1 teaspoon laurel (also called bay leaf)
- 1 teaspoon oregano
- 1 teaspoon basil
- 1 teaspoon thyme
- 1 teaspoon mint
- 1 bunch of parsley, chopped
- 1 bunch of dill, chopped

How to Prepare:

1. Set your Instant Pot to sauté mode and add some sunflower oil.
2. Add the chili pepper powder and sauté for 5 minutes.
3. Add the onion, 2 tablespoons of cilantro, garlic and season with the salt and pepper.
4. Stir for a few minutes and add the fish stock.
5. Season the salmon heads with the salt and pepper and marinate for at least few hours unrefrigerated at room temperature.
6. In the Instant Pot, combine the ¼ cup of cilantro, 1 teaspoon rosemary, 1 teaspoon laurel (also called bay leaf), 1 teaspoon oregano, 1 teaspoon basil, 1 teaspoon thyme, 1 teaspoon mint, 1

bunch of parsley and all the remaining ingredients and the salmon
heads.

7. Close the lid and cook on a LOW pressure for 65 minutes.

8. Release the pressure over 10 minutes.

9. Portion the soup into four bowls or mugs and dollop each bowl
with the chopped dill. Remember that this dish should be served
warm.

<u>Nutrition (Per Serving):</u>
Calories: 264; Fat: 54g; Carbohydrates: 174g; Protein: 42g

Omelet with Walnuts and Salmon

Serving: 2
Prep Time: 15 minutes
Cooking Time: 40 minutes

Ingredients:

- 6 eggs
- 1 baguette
- 10 oz salmon, diced
- 2 oz walnuts
- 3 medium onions, chopped
- 3 tablespoon Olive oil
- ½ cup of milk
- 2 teaspoons dry onions
- 2 tablespoons unsalted butter or baking spray
- 1 teaspoon herbs
- salt, to taste
- pepper, to taste

How to Prepare:

1. Grease the ramekin with the unsalted butter or baking spray and add in the onions.

2. In a bowl, beat the eggs, milk and the salt using an electric hand mixer until there is a smooth and creamy consistency and homogenous mass.
3. Cut the baguette into small cubes and toss them with the salt, Olive oil, herbs and onion powder. Preheat the oven to 250°-270° Fahrenheit and place the baguette cubes on a baking sheet. Bake the croutons for 10-15 minutes until golden brown and crispy.
4. Combine all the ingredients with the croutons and pour the eggs mixture into the ramekin.
5. Add some water to your pot and place a steamer basket.
6. Then place the ramekin inside and close the lid.
7. Cook on a LOW pressure for 25 minutes and then release the pressure naturally.
8. Sprinkle the walnuts and you are free to serve the omelet in separate dishes with the coffee. Remember that this dish should be served warm.

Nutrition (Per Serving)
Calories: 217; Fat: 24g; Carbohydrates: 34g; Protein: 24g

Spicy Jalapeno Tuna Steak with Lime and Tomato Paste

Serving: 2
Prep Time: 5 minutes
Cook Time: 35 minutes

Ingredients:

- 1 pound of tuna steak, sliced
- 4 small limes, peeled and sliced
- 2 onions, peeled and chopped
- 1 tablespoon of ginger, minced
- 1 jalapeno pepper, chopped
- 5 tablespoons sunflower oil
- 4 garlic cloves, minced
- 4 tablespoon shredded coconut
- 5 tablespoons tomato sauce

How to Prepare:

1. In a bowl, combine the onions, jalapeno pepper, garlic, ginger and tomato paste. Toss the fish steak in the spices. Then set the steak aside to marinate it for at least few hours unrefrigerated at room temperature or place in the fridge overnight.
2. Set your Instant Pot to sauté mode and add in the sunflower oil and limes.
3. Allow the oil to heat up and add the skirt steak and stir for about 2 minutes.
4. Close the lid to cook on a HIGH pressure for 35 minutes.
5. Garnish with shredded coconut and serve!

Nutrition (Per Serving):
Calories: 368; Fat: 81g; Carbohydrates: 264g; Protein: 66g

Cod and Zucchini Stew

Serving: 3
Prep Time: 10 minutes
Cooking Time: 60 minutes

Ingredients:

- 3 cod fillets
- 1 medium zucchini, spiralized
- 1 cup of fish broth
- 1 cup of water
- 1 cup of tomatoes, chopped
- 3 teaspoons basil, dried and crushed
- 1 green bell pepper, seeded and cubed
- 1/8 teaspoon oregano, crushed
- ½ medium onion, chopped
- 4 garlic cloves, minced
- sea salt and black pepper, to taste

How to Prepare:

1. Spiralize the zucchini or use the Korean carrot grater.
2. Marinate the fish in oregano, garlic, salt and pepper. Then set the cod aside to marinate for at least few hours unrefrigerated at room temperature or place in the fridge overnight.
3. Add all the ingredients to the Instant Pot and mix well.
4. Close the lid and select the slow mode to cook for 60 minutes.
5. Keep the pressure and then release the handle to the Venting position.
6. Once cooked, stir the stew well.
7. Portion the fish into bowls or mugs. Remember that this dish should be served warm. Serve it with the buckwheat.

Nutrition (Per Serving):

Calories: 281; Fat: 58g; Carbohydrates: 179g; Protein: 48g

Salmon, Shrimps and Ramen Coconut Soup

Serving: 3
Prep Time: 10 minutes
Cooking Time: 60 minutes

Ingredients:

- 10 oz salmon, cubed
- 2 cups of shrimps
- 1 cup of coconut milk
- 1 cup of Japanese Ramen noodles
- 3 tablespoons frozen vegetable mix
- 5 cups of water
- 3 teaspoons basil, dried and crushed
- 1/8 teaspoon oregano, crushed
- ½ medium onion, chopped
- 4 garlic cloves, minced
- sea salt and black pepper, to taste

How to Prepare:
1. Add all the ingredients to the Instant Pot and mix well.
2. Close the lid and select the slow mode to cook for 60 minutes.
3. Keep the pressure and then release the handle to the Venting position.

4. Once cooked, stir the soup well.

5. Portion the soup into three bowls or mugs. Remember that this dish should be served warm.

Nutrition (Per Serving):

Calories: 276; Fat: 56g; Carbohydrates: 184g; Protein: 49g

Salmon Curry with Champignons and Gouda

Serving: 4
Prep Time: 15 minutes
Cooking Time: 40 minutes

Ingredients:

- 2 salmon fillets, cubed
- ¾ cup of chickpeas
- 1 cup of champignons, sliced up
- 1 cup of Gouda, grated
- 1 medium onion, peeled and chopped
- 2 garlic cloves, minced
- 1 green chili, seeded and diced
- 1 tablespoon ginger
- ½ a tablespoon turmeric
- 1 can of coconut milk
- 1 cup of vegetable stock
- 3 tablespoons red curry paste
- 2 teaspoons salt
- 1 teaspoon cumin
- ½ teaspoon curry powder
- ¼ teaspoon ground fenugreek
- ¼ teaspoon black pepper
- 1 tablespoon tomato paste
- 3 tablespoons freshly squeezed lemon juice
- 1 cup of spinach, chopped

How to Prepare:

1. Set the pot to sauté mode and add the champignons to the inner pot to cook for 10 minutes.
2. Add in the onion and mix well, cook until clear and caramelized.
3. Add the chili, garlic, ginger, turmeric and sauté for 1-2 minutes.
4. Add all the remaining ingredients with the coconut milk and cancel the sauté mode.
5. Close the lid and cook on a HIGH pressure for 30 minutes.
6. Release the pressure naturally.
7. Stir in the tomato paste, spinach and lemon juice.

8. Portion the curry into four bowls or mugs and dollop each bowl
with the grated Gouda cheese. Remember that this dish should
be served warm.

<u>Nutrition (Per Serving):</u>
Calories: 191; Fat: 42g; Carbohydrates: 182g; Protein: 32g

Spicy Coconut Tuna

Serving: 3
Prep Time: 15 minutes
Cooking Time: 40 minutes
Ingredients:

- 15 oz tuna, cubed
- 1 cup of apricots
- 1 red onion, peeled and chopped
- 2 garlic cloves, minced
- 1 green chili, seeded and diced
- 1 tablespoon ginger
- ½ a tablespoon turmeric
- 1 can of coconut milk
- 1 cup of vegetable stock
- 3 tablespoons red curry paste
- 2 teaspoons salt
- 1 teaspoon cumin
- ½ teaspoon curry powder
- ¼ teaspoon ground fenugreek
- ¼ teaspoon black pepper
- 1 tablespoon tomato paste
- 3 tablespoons freshly squeezed lemon juice
- 1 bunch of chives, chopped

How to Prepare:

1. Wash and soak the apricots in the warm water for 10 minutes.
2. Set the pot to sauté mode and add in the onion to cook for 5 minutes, cook until clear and caramelized.
3. Add in the chili, garlic, ginger, turmeric and sauté for 5 minutes.
4. Add all the remaining ingredients with the coconut milk and cancel the sauté mode.
5. Close the lid and cook for 30 minutes on a HIGH pressure.
6. Release the pressure naturally.
7. Portion the tuna into three bowls or mugs and dollop each bowl with the chopped chives. Serve with the brown rice. Remember that this dish should be served warm.

<u>Nutrition (Per Serving):</u>
Calories: 175; Fat: 37g; Carbohydrates: 220g; Protein: 32g

Pumpkin and Pork Escallops

Serving: 2
Prep Time: 10 minutes
Cooking Time: 40 minutes

Ingredients:

- 40 oz pork, ground
- 1 medium-sized pumpkin, peeled and deseeded, gently cut into eighths
- 4 tablespoons dried sage
- 2 tablespoons clarified and unsalted butter
- 2 teaspoons dried thyme
- 2 teaspoons ground cinnamon
- 1 cup of fish broth

- 1 teaspoon of salt
- 1 teaspoon pepper

How to Prepare:

1. First, set your Instant Pot to sauté mode and melt the unsalted butter or use the skillet to melt the butter and then pour into your Instant Pot.

2. In a bowl, combine the salt, pepper, dried thyme, sage and cinnamon. Season the pork with the spices mix. Form the pork escallops. Add them into the Instant Pot.

3. Then, add in the pumpkin and pour in the fish broth.

4. Close the lid and cook on a HIGH pressure for about 40 minutes.

5. Quick-release the pressure and transfer the pork escallops to a plate.

6. Combine the pumpkin with the pork escallops and ladle up the sauce (if any) all over the meat. Remember that this dish should be served warm. Serve it with the red or white wine.

Nutrition (Per Serving):

Calories: 254; Fat: 63g; Carbohydrates: 199g; Protein: 57g

Pork and Beef with Oranges

Serving: 4
Prep Time: 25 minutes
Cooking Time: 65 minutes

Ingredients:

- 20 oz pork, cubed
- 20 oz beef, cubed
- 2 oranges, peeled and diced
- 2 bacon slices
- 1 garlic clove, minced
- 1 medium onion, chopped
- 2 medium carrots, chopped
- 1 bunch of parsley, chopped
- 1 tablespoon thyme
- ½ a cup beef stock
- ½ cup red wine
- 1 large potato, cubed
- ½ a tablespoon olive oil
- Salt and pepper to taste

How to Prepare:

1. In a bowl, combine the garlic, parsley, salt and pepper. Toss the pork and beef in the spices and vegetables mix. Then pour the wine on top and set the pork and beef aside to marinate them for at least few hours unrefrigerated at room temperature or place in the fridge overnight.

2. Set your pot to sauté mode and pour the oil, allow the oil to heat up.

3. Add the pork and beef cubes and cook for 15 minutes.

4. Transfer the pork and beef into a plate.

5. Add in the bacon and onion and sauté until translucent and caramelized. Then mix in all the vegetables and sauté for 20 minutes.

6. Add in the pork and beef and all the remaining ingredients.

7. Close the lid and cook for 30 minutes on a HIGH pressure.

8. Release the pressure naturally over 10 minutes.

9. Then portion the meat into four plates and top each plate with the cooked vegetables. Remember that this dish should be served warm. Serve it with the beer.

<u>Nutrition (Per Serving):</u>
Calories: 392; Fat: 86g; Carbohydrates: 285g; Protein: 89g

Pork Curry with Cheese

Serving: 4
Prep Time: 15 minutes
Cooking Time: 40 minutes

Ingredients:

- 20 oz pork, cubed
- 1 cup of champignons, sliced up
- 1 cup of Parmesan cheese, grated
- 1 medium onion, peeled and chopped
- 2 garlic cloves, minced
- 1 green chili, seeded and diced
- 1 tablespoon ginger
- ½ a tablespoon turmeric
- 1 cup of vegetable stock
- 3 tablespoons red curry paste
- 2 teaspoons salt
- 1 teaspoon cumin
- ½ teaspoon curry powder
- ¼ teaspoon ground fenugreek
- ¼ teaspoon black pepper
- 1 tablespoon tomato paste
- 3 tablespoons freshly squeezed lemon juice
- 1 cup of spinach, chopped

How to Prepare:

1. Set the pot to sauté mode and add the champignons to the inner pot to cook for 10 minutes.
2. Add in the onion and mix well, cook until clear and caramelized.
3. Add the chili, garlic, ginger, turmeric and sauté for 1-2 minutes.
4. Add all the remaining ingredients and cancel the sauté mode.
5. Close the lid and cook on a HIGH pressure for around 40 minutes.
6. Release the pressure naturally.
7. Stir in the tomato paste, spinach and lemon juice.

8. Portion the curry into four bowls or mugs and dollop each bowl
    with the grated Parmesan cheese. Remember that this dish
    should be served warm.

<u>Nutrition (Per Serving):</u>
Calories: 247; Fat: 45g; Carbohydrates: 213g; Protein: 35g

Pork Belly in Beer

Serving: 3
Prep Time: 10 minutes
Cooking Time: 50 minutes

Ingredients:

- 20 oz pork belly
- 1 cup of onions, peeled and chopped
- 1 cup of orange juice
- 3 tablespoons avocado oil
- 4 garlic cloves, minced
- ¼ teaspoon red pepper flakes
- 3 teaspoons sesame seeds

How to Prepare:

1. In a bowl, combine the belly, pepper, onions, tomato sauce, garlic, oil, pepper flakes and sesame seeds and toss well. Pour the beer and marinate the pork for at least few hours unrefrigerated at room temperature or place in the fridge overnight. Add it to your instant pot and close the lid to cook on a HIGH pressure for around 40 minutes.
2. Open the lid and place the pork on the cutting board and slice it.

3. Return the pork to the instant pot and set your instant pot to sauté mode.

4. Cook the pork for 10 minutes and portion it into three plates and dollop each plate with some sesame seeds. Remember that this dish should be served warm.

Nutrition (Per Serving):
Calories: 223; Fat: 48g; Carbohydrates: 189g; Protein: 42g

Zucchini and Pork Meat

Serving: 2
Prep Time: 10 minutes
Cooking Time: 55 minutes

Ingredients:

- 2 pieces of ½ inch thick bone-in pork loin or rib
- 1 medium zucchini, peeled and diced
- 4 tablespoons dried sage
- 2 tablespoons clarified and unsalted butter
- 2 teaspoons dried thyme
- 2 teaspoons ground cinnamon
- 1 cup of beef broth
- 1 teaspoon of salt
- 1 teaspoon pepper

How to Prepare:

1. First, set your Instant Pot to sauté mode and melt the unsalted butter or use the skillet to melt the butter and then pour it into your Instant Pot.
2. In a bowl, combine the salt, pepper, dried thyme, sage and cinnamon. Season the pork meat with the spices mix and toss it in the unsalted butter to cook for 10 minutes.
3. Then, add in the zucchini and pour in the beef broth.
4. Close the lid and cook on a HIGH pressure for about 45 minutes.
5. Quick-release the pressure and transfer the pork to a plate.
6. Spoon the zucchini around the pork nicely and ladle up the sauce (if any) all over the pork. Remember that this dish should be served warm. Serve it with the cold beer.

Nutrition (Per Serving):
Calories: 385; Fat: 79g; Carbohydrates: 282g; Protein: 75g

Instant Pork with Cabbage

Serving: 2
Prep Time: 15 minutes
Cooking Time: 55 minutes

Ingredients:

- 25 oz pork, ground
- ½ large onion, chopped
- 1 cabbage, chopped
- 1 cup of peanuts
- 1 garlic clove, minced
- 1 bay leaf
- 2 ounces tomato sauce
- 1 tablespoon olives, pitted
- 1 tablespoon cilantro, chopped
- ½ cup of water
- 2 teaspoon chili powder
- Salt and pepper, to taste

How to Prepare:

1. Preheat the oven to 240°-260°Fahrenheit and roast the peanuts in the oven for 10 minutes until lightly browned and crispy and then set aside to cool completely. Then grind the peanuts using a food processor or blender.
2. Marinate the pork in the salt, pepper and chili powder for at least few hours unrefrigerated at room temperature or place in the fridge overnight. Set the Instant Pot to sauté mode and add in the pork. Break the pork meat into pieces and cook until browned.
3. Add in all the remaining ingredients and mix well.
4. Close the lid and cook for 45 minutes on a HIGH pressure.
5. Then portion the pork into two plates. Remember that this dish should be served warm. Serve it with the salad and brown rice.

Nutrition (Per Serving):

Calories: 380; Fat: 76g; Carbohydrates: 280g; Protein: 68g

Pork in Tomato Sauce with Pineapple

Serving: 3
Prep Time: 15 minutes
Cooking Time: 55 minutes

Ingredients:

- 5 pieces 2-inch pork
- 1 cup of pineapple, cubed
- 1 cup of tomato sauce
- 4 ounces pancetta, diced
- 2 teaspoons pepper
- 2 carrots, peeled and chopped
- 3 teaspoons dried rosemary
- 4 teaspoons garlic, minced
- ½ cup of orange juice
- ¼ cup of chicken broth
- soy sauce, to taste

How to Prepare:

1. In a bowl, combine the pepper, dried rosemary and garlic. Toss the pork in the spices mix. Then set the pork aside to marinate it for at least few hours unrefrigerated at room temperature or place in the fridge overnight.

2. Combine all the ingredients in your Instant Pot and close the lid to let them cook for about 55 minutes on a HIGH pressure.

3. Release the pressure quickly and transfer the pork to a carving board.

4. Slice up the meat into strips. Divide into three plates and pour the soy sauce on top to serve.

Nutrition (Per Serving):

Calories: 382; Fat: 82g; Carbohydrates: 286g; Protein: 74g

Pork and Pancetta in Tomato Sauce with Butter

Serving: 3
Prep Time: 15 minutes
Cooking Time: 50 minutes

Ingredients:

- 5 pieces 2-inch pork
- 1 cup of tomato sauce
- 4 ounces pancetta, diced
- 4 tablespoons salted butter
- 1 medium shallot, chopped
- 5 garlic cloves, minced
- 3 teaspoons dried rosemary
- 2 teaspoons black pepper
- 1 teaspoon nutmeg
- 1 cup of chicken broth

How to Prepare:

1. In a bowl, combine the black pepper, dried rosemary, nutmeg and garlic. Toss the pork in the spices mix. Then set the pork aside to marinate it for at least few hours unrefrigerated at room temperature or place in the fridge overnight.

2. Set your pot to sauté mode and add in the pancetta to cook for about 5 minutes.

3. Then transfer the browned up pancetta to a plate.

4. Add shallots and cook for 5 minutes.

5. Combine all the ingredients in you Instant Pot and close the lid to let them cook on a HIGH pressure for about 40 minutes.

6. Release the pressure and place the pork to a carving board.

7. Slice up the meat into strips and then divide into three bowls or plates and ladle up the tomato sauce and then spoon some salted butter on top to serve with the white bread and wine.

Nutrition (Per Serving):

Calories: 393; Fat: 92g; Carbohydrates: 293g; Protein: 89g

Honey Pork with Oranges

Serving: 2
Prep Time: 10 minutes
Cook Time: 45 minutes

Ingredients:

- 20 oz pork
- 4 oranges, peeled and diced
- 5 tablespoons liquid honey
- 2 tablespoon Gouda cheese, grated
- 2 tablespoons soy sauce
- 1 tablespoon dry basil
- 5 garlic cloves, minced
- 4 tablespoons olive oil
- Salt as needed
- 1 cup of freshly squeezed orange juice
- ½ tablespoon of corn starch
- ½ cup of water

How to Prepare:

1. Marinate the pork in the salt, soy sauce, dry basil, minced garlic, orange juice and honey for at least few hours unrefrigerated at room temperature or place in the fridge overnight. Add the marinated pork and all the listed ingredients to your Instant Pot.
2. Close the lid, set the timer to 45 minutes and cook the pork on MEAT/STEW mode.
3. Release the pressure naturally over 10 minutes.
4. Serve and enjoy!

Nutrition (Per Serving):
Calories: 379; Fat: 74g; Carbohydrates: 277g; Protein: 64g

Pork Steak with Kale

Serving: 3
Prep Time: 10 minutes
Cook Time: 60 minutes
<u>**Ingredients:**</u>

- 3 pork steaks
- 3 pears, sliced
- 3 tablespoons melted butter
- 3 kale leaves
- 2 tablespoons apple cider
- ½ teaspoon ground black pepper
- 2 medium yellow onions, peeled and cut into 8 wedges
- ½ teaspoon ground allspice
- 1 teaspoon black pepper

<u>**How to Prepare:**</u>

1. In a skillet, melt the butter and set your Instant Pot to sauté mode and spoon the melted butter.
2. Add in the pork steaks and sauté for around 20 minutes.
3. Transfer the meat to a plate.

4. Add in the onion and pears in the Instant Pot and allow them to sauté for 10 minutes until the onions are slightly browned and caramelized.

5. Add in the pork and pour the apple cider on top. Combine all the ingredients (except kale) and close the lid to cook on a HIGH pressure for 20-30 minutes.

6. Portion the pork into the three plates. Remember that this dish should be served warm. Serve the pork with the fresh kale.

<u>Nutrition (Per Serving):</u>
Calories: 378; Fat: 77g; Carbohydrates: 275g; Protein: 64g

Spicy Pork Shoulder with Brown Rice

Serving: 4
Prep Time: 10 minute
Cook Time: 65 minutes

Ingredients:

- 30 oz pork shoulder, cut into half
- 1 cup of brown rice
- 1 cup of water
- 5 tablespoons sunflower oil
- salt and pepper to taste
- 1 tablespoon liquid smoke
- steamed green beans or brown rice for serving (optional)
- 2 teaspoons chili pepper powder

How to Prepare:

1. Wash the brown rice several times and boil the water to cook the rice for about 20 minutes or follow the cooking time suggested on the packet. Add 2 tablespoons sunflower oil when the rice is ready.
2. Set your Instant Pot to sauté mode and pour some oil to heat it up.
3. Add in the pork, salt, chili pepper powder and pepper, brown each side for 5 minutes until the both sides are slightly browned. Transfer them to a plate.
4. Pour the water and liquid smoke to the Instant Pot and place the meat and spoon the rice.
5. Close the lid and cook for 60 minutes on a HIGH pressure, release pressure naturally over 10 minutes.
6. Transfer the pork meat to the cutting board and shred using 2 forks. Portion the pork into four plates and dollop each plate with the cooking liquid. Remember that this dish should be served warm. Serve it with the rice on the side.

Nutrition (Per Serving):
Calories: 384; Fat: 75g; Carbohydrates: 275g; Protein: 64g

Pork Ribs with Honey

Serving: 2
Prep Time: 10 minutes
Cooking Time: 50 minutes

Ingredients:

- 15 oz pork back ribs
- 2 tablespoons honey
- 1 teaspoon sesame oil
- 2 tablespoons oyster sauce
- 1 teaspoon salt
- 1 teaspoon sugar
- 1 cup of water
- ½ cup of liquid smoke

How to Prepare:

1. In a bowl, marinate the pork back ribs in honey. Then set the meat aside to marinate for at least few hours unrefrigerated at room temperature or place in the fridge overnight.
2. Add all the listed ingredients to the Instant Pot.
3. Close the lid and cook on MEAT/STEW mode for 50 minutes.
4. Release the pressure naturally over 10 minutes.
5. Portion the pork ribs into two plates and dollop each plate with the cooking liquid and oyster sauce. Remember that this dish should be served warm. Serve it with the buckwheat or brown rice on the side if you prefer.

Nutrition (Per Serving):
Calories: 364; Fat: 70g; Carbohydrates: 264g; Protein: 76g

Jamaican Style Pork with Rice

Serving: 3
Prep Time: 10 minutes
Cooking Time: 60 minutes
Ingredients:

- 1 pound pork, cubed
- 2 cups of rice
- 2 tablespoons Jamaican jerk spice blend
- 1 tablespoon unsalted butter
- ½ cup vegetables broth
- 5 tablespoons Olive oil
- 3 tablespoons lemon or lime juice

How to Prepare:

1. Soak the rice in the warm water overnight. Wash the rice several times and boil the water to cook the rice for about 20 minutes or follow the cooking time suggested on the packet. Add 2 tablespoons Olive oil when the rice is ready.
2. Pour some Olive oil over the pork.
3. Sprinkle the Jamaican spice blend on all sides and marinate the pork in the spices for at least few hours unrefrigerated at room temperature or place in the fridge overnight.

4. Set your Instant Pot to sauté mode and add in the unsalted butter.
5. Add in the pork and brown on all sides for around 10-15 minutes.
6. Then pour the vegetables broth over the pork.
7. Close the lid and cook for 45 minutes on a HIGH pressure.
8. Release the pressure naturally over 10 minutes.
9. Portion the pork into three plates and dollop each plate with the cooking liquid. Combine it with the rice and serve warm.

Nutrition (Per Serving):
Calories: 367; Fat: 75g; Carbohydrates: 263g; Protein: 67g

Pork and Parsley Omelet with Onions

Serving: 3

Prep Time: 10 minutes

Cooking Time: 25 minutes

Ingredients:

- 6 eggs
- 20 oz smoked pork meat, cubed
- a drizzle of olive oil
- 2 onions, peeled and chopped
- 1 medium red onion, peeled and chopped
- salt and black pepper, to taste
- 1 bunch of parsley, chopped

How to Prepare:

1. Beat the eggs using an electric hand mixer until there is a creamy consistency and homogenous mass.
2. In a frying pan or wok, heat the olive oil and fry the chopped red onion and white onions with the pork meat for 5-10 minutes until clear and caramelized.
3. In a bowl, mix the eggs with the salt, pepper, meat and onions and whisk them well.
4. Set the Pot on sauté mode.
5. Add some olive oil and then heat it up and slightly pour the egg mixture. Mix the eggs mixture well.
6. Press the Air Crisp mode and cook the eggs for 15 minutes at 250° Fahrenheit.
7. Portion the omelet into plates and dollop each plate with the chopped parsley. Remember that this dish should be served warm. Serve the omelet with the tea and toasts.

Nutrition (Per Serving):

Calories: 262; Fat: 38g; Carbohydrates: 63g; Protein: 34g

Sausages Omelet with Bread and Peanuts
Serving: 4

Prep Time: 10 minutes

Cooking Time: 35 minutes

Ingredients:

- 8 eggs
- 25 oz smoked pork sausages, sliced
- 1 cup of peanuts
- 25 oz bread, diced
- 2 tablespoons olive oil
- 2 medium carrots, peeled and diced
- 1 medium onion, peeled and chopped
- salt and black pepper, to taste
- 1 bunch of parsley

How to Prepare:

1. Beat the eggs using an electric hand mixer until there is a creamy consistency and homogenous mass.
2. In a frying pan or wok, heat the olive oil and fry the bread for 10 minutes until golden brown and crispy. Then add in the sausages and chopped onion and fry for 5-10 minutes until clear and caramelized.
3. In a bowl, mix the eggs with the salt, pepper, salmon, bread and onion and whisk them well.
4. Set the Pot on sauté mode.
5. Add some olive oil and then heat it up and slightly pour the egg mixture. Stir the eggs mixture well.
6. Press the Air Crisp mode and cook the eggs for 15 minutes at 250° Fahrenheit.
7. Portion the omelet into bowls and dollop each bowl with the chopped parsley and peanuts. Remember that this dish should be served warm. Serve the omelet with the coffee and toasts.

Nutrition (Per Serving):

Calories: 257; Fat: 36g; Carbohydrates: 65g; Protein: 31g

Conclusion

Thank you for buying this Instant Pot cookbook. I hope this cookbook was able to help you to prepare fresh and healthy Instant Pot recipes.

If you are new in this field of Instant Pot cuisine, this book will help you to start your cooking journey. The recipes in this book are simple, and the process of cooking and preparing dishes is explained in the simple way. We also added some more complex recipes. Those you can cook, when you level of experience will grow and you will feel more confident. But never give up, always be open to learn and try something new!

If you've enjoyed this Instant Pot cookbook, I'd greatly appreciate if you could leave an honest review on Amazon. Reviews are very important to us authors, and it only takes a minute for you to post.

Your direct feedback could be used to help other readers to discover the advantages of Instant Pot recipes!

If you have success story, please send it to me! I'm always happy to hear about my reader's success!

If you have anything you want me to know, any questions, suggestions or feedback, please don't hesitate to contact me.

Thank you again and I hope you have enjoyed this cookbook.

4 2 6 1 6 9 0 1 *